8/22/2022

Also surprised I found a copy of this!

Life's Little Instruction Book®

from

Mothers to Daughters

H. Jackson Brown, Jr., and Kim Shea

Much love,
Lynn

D0897513

Rutledge Hill Press™
Nashville, Tennessee
A Division of Thomas Nelson, Inc.
www.ThomasNelson.com

Kim's Dedication

To my mother
who taught me how to love
To my grandmothers
who taught me how to love forever
To my daughters
who have given me four perfect reasons to do both

Life's Little Instruction Book is a registered trademark of H. Jackson Brown, Jr.

Published by Rutledge Hill Press, a division of Thomas Nelson, Inc., P.O. Box 141000, Nashville, Tennessee 37214.

Cover design by Southern Draw Design

Library of Congress Cataloging-in-Publication Data
Brown. H. Jackson, 1940–
    Mothers to daughters / H. Jackson Brown, Jr. and Kim Shea.
        p. cm. — (Life's little instruction books)
    ISBN 1-55853-832-1 (pbk.)
    1. Mothers and daughters—Quotations, maxims, etc. 2. Daughters—Quotations, maxims, etc. I. Shea, Kim, 1962– II. Title. III. Series.

HQ755.85 .B76 2000
306.874'3—dc21   00-062683

Printed in the United States of America
3 4 5 6 7 8 9—06 05 04 03 02

www.Instructionbook.com

JACKSON'S INTRODUCTION

IT WAS JUST AN AVERAGE morning until I opened an envelope postmarked Beaverton, Michigan. It was a short two-paragraph letter, but the contents set in motion a new friendship and a two-year collaboration.

The letter was from a young mother of two daughters (now four) who had recently read and enjoyed my *Life's Little Instruction Book* series. She wrote to say that it was the inspiration for a collection of words of advice she was writing for her daughters. She included thirty-nine sample entries and asked my opinion and if I would like to see more.

My reaction was immediate. Now two years later, I still vividly recall three of the entries that jumped off the page and into my heart:

1. Dive for the bouquet.
2. Drive a tractor.
3. Feed a calf with a bottle.

Wow! What a spontaneous and spirited way of seeing the world. I called that afternoon to tell Kim that I appreciated the letter and admired both the freshness and the soundness of her insights. I encouraged her to "keep at it" and offered to help any way I could. We eventually decided to work together on the project as co-authors and this little book offering time-tested mother-to-daughter perspectives is the result.

Obviously I'm not a mother, nor even a father of a daughter, but that hasn't prevented me from adding to Kim's list with observations of my own. So don't be surprised if some instructions sound a bit stern and direct. Those probably are my contributions; the ones you'll like best and want to remember are Kim's.

H. Jackson Brown, Jr.
August, 2000
Tall Pine Lodge

Kim's Introduction

IT WAS a chilly Sunday afternoon. Cassaday Ann, three years old then, was snuggled up in a nest of favorite blankets in the middle of the family room floor, napping in her church clothes. As my husband, Mike, and I lovingly watched her sleep, we knew that this moment would be one we would store always in our hearts and in our memories. I wanted to bottle up this one peaceful Sunday afternoon nap so that we could open it at any point in Cassaday's life and remember the angelic peacefulness of her youth.

But as we looked at her, I knew that these precious moments were fleeting and that the time would come all too soon when her three-year-old dreams would grow into a world of bicycles, books, and boyfriends. We would soon experience the anxieties and pressures of her teen years, the excitement and adventures of college, careers, and perhaps even the joy of her becoming a mother herself one day. I knew that we could not always be with her to protect and guide her throughout this journey, but I could offer her the protection and guidance of what I had learned. I wanted to share with her insights that would help her reach her dreams in the years ahead, whether as a seven-year-old girl or as a thirty-seven-year-old mother. And so I began to write down some of the observations of life that had helped me become who I am.

The simple insights on the following pages began as the heartfelt words of advice I first wrote down that day and have been collecting throughout the years. I have written them not only with Cassaday Ann in mind, but now also Kennedy Jo, Clarity Grace, and Century Eva—Cassaday's three younger sisters.

I hope you will enjoy this collection of loving wisdom and that you will also live it. But most importantly, I hope you will share it with the people most precious in your life.

Kim Shea
August, 2000
Beaverton, Michigan

The author with her daughters at home.
Left to Right: Cassaday Ann, Kennedy Jo,
Clarity Grace, Kim, and Century Eva.

1 • Be the person you'd be proud of your daughter becoming.

2 • Form good habits. They are as hard to break as bad ones.

3 • Never do anything that would cause you to lose the trust and affection of your husband and children.

4 • Remember the three essentials of a happy household: prayer, patience and praises.

5 • Stand up for what you believe even if you have to stand alone.

6 • Devote time to your child's scrapbook. Today's special moments are tomorrow's treasured memories.

7 • Give more gifts than you receive.

8 • Make sure your children's book collection is larger than their video collection.

9 • As often as you can, give in to the request for "just one more story, Mommy."

10 • Remember that every backyard needs a swing.

11 • Remember that money can't buy happiness; it can only rent it for a while.

12 • When you want to be taken seriously, dress seriously.

13 • Life is a dance. Don't sit it out.

14 • Let your life be your sermon.

15 ◆ Never slam a door in anger. It might be a while before it opens again.

16 ◆ Never order French onion soup on a first date.

17 ◆ Remember that some things are urgent, and others are important. Know the difference.

18 ◆ Praise your children's good decisions and good choices, not their good luck.

19 ◆ Remember that all happy marriages are the result of compromising and forgiving.

20 ◆ When giving a gift to someone who is ill, consider something they can use when they get well.

21 ◆ Sit down in new clothes before cutting off the tags.

22 ◆ When your heart has been broken, put yourself in a situation where it can get broken again. It's the best cure.

23 ◆ Don't expect to be what you haven't worked hard to become.

A mother sets the tone for her daughter's life, provides a road map and a role model, and continues through the daughter's middle and old age to be her example.

—Victoria Secunda

24 ◆ Remember that most marital problems can be solved if you both work on them together.

25 ◆ Identify those things that make you the happiest. Allow yourself time to do them.

26 ◆ Secretly drop a little love note into your husband's coat pocket tomorrow.

27 · Surround yourself with people who support your virtues, not ones who test your vices.

28 ◆ Never open a closed bathroom or bedroom door without knocking.

29 ◆ When traveling, never pack a linen suit.

30 ◆ Always paint your toenails red when wearing a new pair of sandals.

31 ◆ Know how to make a campfire and change a tire.

32 • Kiss your husband passionately in an unexpected moment.

33 • Be the aunt that all of your nieces and nephews refer to as their favorite.

34 • Send a congratulations card to any baby born to people you know (even a little bit). It's a miracle worth recognizing.

35 ◆ Always look the person in the eyes when saying, "I'm sorry."

36 ◆ Always look the person in the eyes when saying, "I forgive you."

37 ◆ Always look the person in the eyes when saying, "I love you."

38 ◆ Overpay good baby-sitters.

39 • Remember that nothing is a bargain if you don't need it.

40 • Never forget the healing power of a good night's sleep.

41 • When searching for the love of your life, remember that you might have to date a lot of lemons before you find the peach.

42 • Always read your hometown paper. Send congratulatory notes to the homecoming queens, valedictorians, and award winners that you know or whose parents you know.

43 • Place a high value on the friends who help you move.

44 • Never stop sharpening your computer skills.

45 • Send lots of Valentines.

46 • Don't be afraid to be the first one to begin applauding. Or the last to stop.

47 • Know your children's friends as well as you know your own.

48 • Remember that wealth and wisdom mean little unless shared.

49 • Look under the cushions of chairs and sofas before you give them away. A misplaced item might be found there.

50 • Perfect the art of forgiveness, as well as the art of apology.

51 • Remember that the size of your heart is the only measurement God cares about.

52 • Pay for those lessons, buy those uniforms, and attend those games.

53 • Welcome new neighbors with a pan of homemade brownies.

54 • Remember that when nothing else comes to mind, you can always compliment a person's eyes or smile.

55 · Don't be in such a hurry
pursuing your dreams that
you rush right past them.

56 ◆ Commission a beautiful drawing of your childhood home as a gift to each of your siblings.

57 ◆ Have a favorite flower, and make sure your husband knows what it is.

58 ◆ Put as much into your day as you hope to get out of it.

59 • Never refuse to answer another question from your inquisitive youngster, no matter how tempting it may be.

60 • Don't "settle" when it comes to the grades you get or the goals you set.

61 • Never give a gift that's not beautifully wrapped.

They always looked back before turning the corner, for their mother was always at the window to nod and smile, and wave her hand at them. Somehow it seemed as if they couldn't have got through the day without that, for whatever their mood might be, the last glimpse of that motherly face was sure to affect them like sunshine.

—Louisa May Alcott

62 • Surround your workspace with pictures drawn by your children.

63 • Expose your children to the arts. Make sure they know that the *theater* is more than big screens and buckets of popcorn.

64 • Never forget that being loved is better than being rich.

65 ◆ Remember that the most treasured antiques are old friends.

66 ◆ If you're trying to decide if someone's action warrants a thank-you note, the answer is always yes.

67 ◆ Savor the words "I love you" each and every time you hear them.

68 ◆ Feed a calf with a bottle.

69 ◆ Keep extra gifts on hand for spur-of-the-moment events.

70 ◆ If someone plans a good surprise for you, act surprised.

71 ◆ Become a favorite customer at your favorite stores.

72 • Never start a diet on a weekend.

73 • Never keep anything from your doctor.

74 • Never make an important decision when you're upset or angry.

75 • Never get serious with a man who has more shoes than you do.

76 ◆ Write to your cousins.

77 ◆ If you're wondering what to do with your afternoon, visit a library or a bookstore.

78 ◆ Create the tradition of serving pancakes with real maple syrup for Saturday breakfasts.

79 ◆ Never ruin an apology with an excuse.

80 • View the ring in the bathtub as evidence that your children had a good day.

81 • Be faithful to your husband, your heart, and your hairdresser.

82 • Dive for the bouquet.

83 • Never say anything in front of a child that you don't want repeated.

84 · Determine your response to temptation long before it taps you on the shoulder.

85 • Hold a newborn baby any time you get the chance.

86 • Add an extra egg and a teaspoon of vanilla to a cake mix to make it taste more like homemade.

87 • Keep personal copies of your grandmother's favorite recipes written in her own handwriting.

88 ◆ Every once in a while, let your boss see you sweat.

89 ◆ Volunteer to teach a Sunday School class.

90 ◆ Spend the money necessary to ensure that your children have beautiful, straight teeth.

91 ◆ When the choice is available, buy hardcover over paperback.

92 • Be the person your friends refer to as their best friend.

93 • Don't waste today worrying about yesterday.

94 • To keep from misplacing your keys or purse, put them in the same place every time you enter your house.

95 ◆ Teach your children to pray. There are no sweeter words than "God bless Mommy and God bless Daddy."

96 ◆ To pull yourself out of a low moment, start by holding your head up high.

97 ◆ Never pass up an opportunity to hold your dad's hand, regardless of your age.

98 • Never find fault in the contributions of people who volunteer their time.

99 • Carry a list in your wallet of the medicines you and your family are allergic to.

100 • Don't be afraid occasionally to rock the boat.

101 • Remember that happiness depends more on give than on take.

102 • Don't wish your life away. Enjoy the moment and all the blessings that are in it.

103 • Don't consider a bigger water heater an extravagance. You never ever want to run out of hot water.

104 • Drink your morning coffee from the most interesting, brightly colored mug you can find.

105 ◆ Never let your gas gauge drop below a quarter tank.

106 ◆ Keep a $20 bill hidden in your car for emergencies.

107 ◆ When you've decided to give up on something or someone, give it just one more try.

108 · Do more than expected
and no one will ever be
disappointed in you.

109 • Learn to play a sport and a musical instrument reasonably well.

110 • Keep several postage stamps in your billfold.

111 • Surround yourself with people who make you laugh.

112 • Label and file your photographs in a photo album as soon as you bring them home.

113 ✦ Keep a family Bible on the coffee table.
Leave the pages open to your favorite verse.

114 ✦ Warm up a special handshake by using
both hands.

115 ✦ If you go to the movies with someone you
want to be close to, leave your sweater at
home.

116 ◆ Never miss your annual physical.

117 ◆ Plan a slumber party for your nieces. Make it an annual tradition.

118 ◆ Eat lots of warm oatmeal. Don't forget the brown sugar and raisins.

119 ◆ Be nice to the telephone operator.

120 ◆ Remember that a smile is the quickest way to improve your appearance.

121 ◆ Compliment your husband and your children every day.

122 ◆ Own a copy of *It's a Wonderful Life*. Watch it every Christmas and whenever you're feeling low.

123 • Count blessings, not calories.

124 • Pray for our leaders.

125 • Don't buy products that sponsor violent television programs.

126 • Give your children reasons to admire your energy.

127 ◆ Think twice before saying "yes" to a stranger.

128 ◆ Think twice before saying "no" to a friend.

129 ◆ Remember that amazing things happen when you substitute "I can't" with "I'll try."

130 ◆ Never stay more than twenty minutes when visiting a non-family member in the hospital.

Stories first heard at mother's knee are never wholly forgotten—a little spring that never quite dries up in our journey through scorching years.

—Given Ruffing

131 · Consider giving trees as gifts; they're perfect for weddings, showers, new babies, housewarmings, and retirements.

132 · Never miss an opportunity to tell someone you love them.

133 · Have your children draw self-portraits every year on their birthdays.

134 ◆ When traveling, save all the free toiletries offered by hotels and motels and donate them to a women's shelter.

135 ◆ Own a world globe, a good dictionary, and a good thesaurus. Refer to them often.

136 ◆ Stop and watch the wonder of geese flying south.

137 ◆ Say something positive as early as possible every day.

138 ◆ Don't go overboard when planning your wedding. The thousands of dollars and hundreds of hours spent by brides and their mothers trying to create the perfect wedding has never guaranteed a lasting, happy marriage.

139 ◆ Pick field daises and keep them in a Mason jar near your kitchen sink.

140 ◆ Remember that every choice you make either moves you forward or holds you back.

141 ◆ Offer a tip to a hard-working person who normally doesn't receive tips. It will make his or her day.

142 • Remember when dating that handsome is as handsome does.

143 • Never go on a date without cab fare home and coins for a phone call.

144 • Be the person your friends call when they need advice, ideas, or help.

145 • Always take your vacation days.

146 · Always compliment
the cook.

147 • Never miss an opportunity to ride a roller coaster.

148 • Clean out your purse at least once a month.

149 • Find a favorite song to share with your sweetheart.

150 • Never go to bed with dishes in the sink.

151 • Remember that everyone you meet is hungry for a kind word.

152 • Never ride a bike while holding a pizza box.

153 • To get the job you want, excel at the job you have.

154 • Take a nap on a Sunday afternoon.

155 • Surround yourself and your home with living things. God gave us the heart and hands to nurture.

156 • When buying clothes, shoes, or jewelry, remember that if it's cheap, it probably looks it.

157 • Give your daughter or daughter-in-law a book of family recipes at her bridal shower.

158 • Be known for your warm embrace, your thoughtful heart, and your generous spirit.

159 • Make homemade peach ice cream.

160 • Keep a memo pad and pen next to every telephone.

161 • Make new friends but treasure the old.

162 • Remember that good habits are the shortest route to the top.

163 • Don't waste time crying over anything that can't cry back.

164 • Pay close attention to each new person you meet. He or she has the ability to change your life.

165 • Use your fine dining manners even in a fast food restaurant.

166 • Use fun photographs to make great personal note-cards, invitations, and thank-you notes.

167 • Don't forget that men like to receive flowers too.

168 • Wade in a creek every chance you get.

169 • Go camping. Take lots of marshmallows, graham crackers, and Hershey bars.

170 • Always use sunscreen, and plenty of it.

171 • Make visiting your elderly loved ones a priority.

172 • Welcome the wondrous feeling of butterflies in your stomach that new love brings.

173 • Turn off the television. Pull out the Scrabble game.

174 • Fly the flag on the Fourth of July. Make sure your children know why.

175 ◆ When you're a weekend guest, tell your host or hostess exactly when you will be arriving and leaving.

176 ◆ Never argue over the toilet seat. It's not that important.

177 ◆ If you're going to make fun of someone, make sure it's yourself.

178 · Never work for a person
you wouldn't be proud to
introduce to your mother.

179 ◆ Share most of the cookies you make.

180 ◆ Save some of the money you make.

181 ◆ Keep all the promises you make.

182 ◆ Know five memorable places in your hometown where you would be proud to take out-of-town guests.

183 • Look in your family Bible for a list of your ancestors when choosing a name for your expected baby.

184 • Be nice to your sisters. They may turn out to be your best friends.

185 • Let your breakfast table placemats be mismatched ones purchased at favorite vacation sites.

186 • Every once in a while, sit in the front pew.

187 • Learn to bake homemade bread.

188 • Include a joke, cartoon, or special note in your child's lunchbox.

189 • Send flowers to your mother on *your* birthday.

190 • Run away for the weekend. Take your husband. Leave the children.

191 • Keep housework in perspective. Your children will remember how happy their home was, not how spotless.

192 • Learn how to administer CPR and how to perform the Heimlich maneuver.

193 • Never reveal personal information during a telephone call that you didn't initiate.

194 • If friends lose a pet, recognize their loss.

195 • Remember that good taste is usually a matter of less, not more.

196 • Cherish the friend who makes you laugh as well as the one who lets you cry.

197 ◆ Let your best friend hear you refer to her as your best friend.

198 ◆ Recall your favorite childhood memories, then recreate them for your children.

199 ◆ Remember that people forget what you say, and what you do, but they never forget the way you make them feel.

200 • Realize that no house is too small when it is filled with love.

201 • Send a thank-you note to your boss after receiving any raise or performance award.

202 • Remember that it's important to be your children's friend, but more important to be their mother.

Every mother is like Moses. She does not enter the promised land. She prepares a world she will not see.

—Pope Paul VI

203 • Pray for your enemies as well as for your loved ones.

204 • Share the movement of your unborn child with your husband at every opportunity. There is no feeling more precious or joy more complete.

205 • Live within your means even if it means living without your wants.

206 ◆ Stand up to bullies.

207 ◆ Look at disappointment as an opportunity to test your creativity.

208 ◆ Work in a political campaign for a candidate you admire.

209 ◆ Realize that all the good advice in the world is worthless unless you take it.

210 • When your newborn arrives, have a local bakery deliver frosted sugar cookies to the office (either pink or blue) with your baby's name written on them.

211 • When nothing is going well, call your grandmother.

212 • Never let anyone in a group feel left out.

213 • Never use profanity. It diminishes your credibility and authority.

214 • Make sun tea.

215 • Squish mud between your toes.

216 • Take off your watch when you're on vacation.

217 ◆ Don't rush to bail your children out of trouble for which they are responsible.

218 ◆ Listen carefully when the people who know you best say something is a bad idea.

219 ◆ Never forget that it's more important to be beautiful to listen to than to be beautiful to look at.

220 · Teach your children that being a person of good character is even more important than excelling at sports or academics.

221 • Every once in a while, sit on the floor and eat delivered pizza by candlelight.

222 • Use the phrase "I need your help" with your children often. Whether you actually need their help in all cases is unimportant.

223 • Never regret any money spent on books or flowers.

224 ◆ Never run out of peanut butter.

225 ◆ When you see an extraordinarily beautiful sunset, take a few moments to enjoy it.

226 ◆ Learn the rules of the sports your children play.

227 ◆ Remember the three "F's": Forgive, Forget, and Forge Ahead.

228 • Talk about your family history often.
Always be proud of your heritage.

229 • Don't underestimate the therapeutic value
of feeling the earth in your hands.

230 • Be selective with your bumper stickers.
The novelty wears off, but the glue
rarely does.

231 • Be the one who always remembers to bring a camera.

232 • Enjoy the success of others just as you enjoy your own.

233 • Never give a book as a gift without including a special inscription on the inside cover.

234 • Volunteer to keep score when you go bowling.

235 • Remember that when it comes to influencing your children, what you do will always be more important than what you say.

236 • Speak highly of your grandmother. One day you may be blessed with the same title.

237 · Remember that the important thing is not what you have in your life, but whom.

238 • Read *The Conversation Piece* by Bret Nicholaus and Paul Lowrie (a book of thought-provoking questions) with family and friends. It's a great campfire book.

239 • Wherever you go, try to leave it cleaner or happier than before you arrived.

240 • Never buy a bridesmaid's dress thinking you'll ever wear it again.

241 ◆ Don't overschedule your child's activities.

242 ◆ Own something perfect to wear if the employer or date of your dreams requests to see you today.

243 ◆ Remember that as long as you are dreaming, believing, and doing, you can go anywhere from nowhere starting with nothing.

244 • Kiss your children goodnight regardless of their ages.

245 • Don't waste time being jealous.

246 • Master the art of making a beautiful sandwich.

247 • Don't trust skinny Italian chefs.

248 • Drive a tractor.

249 • Few things are as important as they first seem. Ask yourself, "Will this make a difference in my life a year from now?"

250 • Keep an extra roll of film in your purse. Someone will inevitably need it at that wedding, party, or special celebration.

251 • Dust before you vacuum.

252 • Never interrupt a person telling a joke by saying, "Oh, I've heard it before."

253 • Encourage people to like you by liking them first.

254 • Remember that the right path is usually uphill.

255 · When you're angry at your husband, remember that he's the only person your children love as much as they love you.

256 • Keep your priorities straight. If you are too busy to do a favor for a friend, you're too busy.

257 • Refrain from discussing in front of your children how little or how much money you have.

258 • Remember that if you wait to stumble upon success, you may simply stumble.

259 • Relish every rainbow.

260 • Don't let your children hear you speak
unkindly to or about your husband.

261 • For a unique birthday gift for a friend or
relative, order a copy of the newspaper
from the day they were born. Call
1-800-221-3221.

262 ◆ Write down immediately all those cute things that your children say.

263 ◆ Never give a gift that requires batteries without including the batteries.

264 ◆ Choose actions and words by day that allow you to sleep in heavenly peace by night.

Children look in those eyes, listen to that dear voice, notice the feeling of even a single touch that is bestowed upon you by that gentle hand! In after life you may have friends, fond dear friends, but never will you have again the inexpressible love and gentleness lavished upon you, which none but a mother bestows.

—Thomas Macaulay

265 • Attack the problem, not the person.

266 • Remember that today and tomorrow are the good old days that you will one day long for.

267 • Don't waste time defending the things you've done that you know you wouldn't do again.

268 • Remember that everyone you meet wants to be noticed, to be heard, to be appreciated, and to be loved.

269 • When donating an old purse to charity, slip a five-dollar bill inside to give the future owner a nice little surprise.

270 • Be known for giving the neighborhood's best Halloween treats.

271 • Create a dreamy room in which to sleep.

272 • Celebrate with your husband the anniversary of your first date. If possible, spend it the same way you did the first time.

273 • Learn to put your heart on paper. The written word can be much more powerful than the spoken one.

274 • Be proud, but not boastful.

275 • Be confident, but not conceited.

276 • Be strong, but not inflexible.

277 • Be brave, but not reckless.

278 • Remember that character shines, beauty fades.

279 • Accept others as they are. It's a gift you can give to them and to yourself.

280 • Send an encouraging note or card to someone this week.

281 • Do your best to ensure that the last three words anyone in your home hears before falling asleep are "I love you."

282 • Your children will rise to the level of expectation you have for them — so have high ones.

283 • Have a beautiful portrait made of yourself to give to your husband.

284 • Never forget that being a good parent is the greatest advantage you can give your child.

285 • Call someone you love and tell them so.

286 • Consider the consequences of your actions before you take them.

287 • Put your faith to work.

288 • Grant yourself incredible freedom by overcoming the need to please all people all of the time.

289 • Take time to talk to the shy kid in the corner.

290 • When you want to know how you really look, ask a five-year-old.

291 • Never buy a swimsuit thinking you will look great in it if you lose a couple of pounds.

292 • Allow your children to experience the joy of giving. Let them participate in selecting gifts for birthday parties, family members, and teachers.

293 • Learn to accept criticism as gracefully as you accept praise.

294 • Love your sister-in-law as your sister.

295 • Return phone calls the same day that you receive them.

296 • Truly appreciate the gifts in your life. Then watch them multiply.

297 • Whenever you're headed out for an appointment that may involve some waiting time, take along a book.

298 · Be the reason someone
becomes inspired today.

299 ◆ Bundle up in a blanket and sit on your front porch on a cold winter's evening.

300 ◆ Pass on to your boss any letters of recognition that you receive at the workplace.

301 ◆ On car trips, teach your children the capitals of the states.

302 • At least once in your lifetime, get a hug from Mickey Mouse.

303 • Remember that clean kitchen counters and neatly made-up beds can hide a score of housecleaning shortcomings.

304 • When shampooing your hair: lather, rinse, don't repeat.

305 • Take time to get to know people. Resist the temptation to judge them by how they look or what they wear.

306 • Don't display hand towels so fancy that your guests are reluctant to use them.

307 • Be mindful that the phrase, "this too shall pass" applies to the good times as well as the bad.

308 ◆ Be the reason someone has a heartfelt laugh today.

309 ◆ Be thankful that there are as many definitions of success as there are people. If we were all aiming for the same thing, there could be only one winner.

310 ◆ Learn how to make your Grandma's special Christmas cookies.

311 • Be guilty of hanging too many Christmas lights.

312 • Never delete someone from your Christmas card list. Your list should grow every year.

313 • Remember that every little girl needs to find a new doll under the Christmas tree.

314 • Gather the family and read "'Twas the Night Before Christmas" every Christmas Eve.

315 • Remember that socks and underwear don't count as Christmas or birthday presents.

316 • Drink hot cocoa with lots of little marshmallows.

317 • Make snow angels with your children.

318 • Remember that the best cure for cold weather is a warm embrace.

319 • Support your children, but let them fight and win some battles for themselves.

320 • Never allow a friend to cry alone.

321 • Let your daughter watch you put on makeup and get all dressed up.

322 • When hugging, don't be the first to let go.

323 • Buy the battery-operated baby swing.

324 • Never break in new hiking boots on a hike.

I looked on child rearing not only as a work of love and duty but as a profession that was fully as interesting and challenging as any honorable profession in the world and one that demanded the best that I could bring to it.

—Rose Kennedy

325 ◆ When disagreements arise, avoid using the words "never" and "always."

326 ◆ Own something made of cashmere that you wear next to your skin.

327 ◆ Wherever you live, always plant a garden, even if it's only basil and rosemary grown in flower pots on a window sill.

328 • Cherish the stressful, challenging years when your children are small. When looking back, you will consider them to be the best years of your life.

329 • When a friend lets you down, create an opportunity for her to make up for it.

330 • Resist the temptation to tell all you know.

331 ◆ Although it's no longer fashionable, bronze your baby's first pair of shoes.

332 ◆ Research the history of your hometown. Teach it to your kids.

333 ◆ Be confident enough in your résumé and your bra size that neither needs to be even the slightest bit padded.

334 ◆ Be tactful and considerate when quitting a job or breaking up with a boyfriend. You just might want to be welcomed back one day.

335 ◆ Let your kitchen table be the place to gather when friends and family need to soothe their souls.

336 ◆ Bless each day with a generous act.

337 • Learn the details of your parents' and grandparents' love stories. Pass them on.

338 • Visit an Amish community. Buy a loaf of bread, and if you can afford it, a handmade quilt. There is no better quality of either available elsewhere.

339 • Never surrender your dreams.

340 · Don't automatically trust the biggest ad in the yellow pages.

341 ◆ Read the biographies of successful women for inspiration.

342 ◆ Avoid gossip.

343 ◆ Be the reason someone feels admired today.

344 ◆ Let your children be children.

345 • Send thank-you notes within two weeks of receiving the favor or gift.

346 • Never speak negatively about your own physical appearance or features in front of your daughter.

347 • Save your daughter's first dress, first doll, and first drawing.

348 ◆ Own a copy of Louisa May Alcott's *Little Women*. Read it to your daughters.

349 ◆ Never pass up a good garage sale.

350 ◆ Allow your children to select a theme for their birthday parties.

351 ◆ Remain an optimist. You will always have more fun.

352 ◆ Remember that you can live happily anywhere as long as you're with the ones you love.

353 ◆ Once in your lifetime, discover the romantic appeal of a hayloft.

354 ◆ Be a source of optimism for all who know you.

355 • Take photographs of the interiors as well as the exteriors of all the places you live, including your dorm rooms. They will recall priceless memories some day.

356 • Remember that the quality of your life is determined by the choices you make.

357 • Realize that sometimes the best response is to just grin and bear it.

358 • Don't be the friend who forgets to write.

359 • Don't be the friend who forgets to phone.

360 • Don't be the friend who forgets to visit.

361 • Remember that successful parenting is based less on what you do for your children and more on what you teach them to do for themselves.

362 ◆ Pray and read the Bible together as a family.

363 ◆ Take your children with you when you go to vote.

364 ◆ Use your best silver and china for your family. They are the most important guests you will ever serve at your table.

365 ◆ Never blow out a birthday candle or witness a falling star without making a wish.

366 ◆ Keep a basket on the handlebars of your bike to collect all the treasures you find.

367 ◆ Develop the relationship with your own brothers and sisters that you'd like your children to have one day with each other.

368 ◆ Make a list of the ways you and your sister are alike. Refer to it the next time you are angry with her.

369 ◆ Remember that when you grow old with the one you love, your love will never grow old.

370 ◆ Slow dance with your husband at every opportunity.

371 · Remember that children need loving the most when they are the hardest to love.

372 ◆ Never underestimate the power of a little black dress and a strand of real pearls.

373 ◆ Remember, you may be only one person to the world, but you may be the world to one person.

374 ◆ Accept the fact that the only person you can be sure of changing is yourself.

375 • Learn the medical history of women on both sides of your family.

376 • Give your children chores and make sure that they are done well and on time.

377 • Remember that life's most important events are sometimes disguised as ordinary moments.

378 ◆ Take photographs of your children on their first day of every school year.

379 ◆ Measure your success as a parent not by what your children are accomplishing, but by the kind of people they are becoming.

380 ◆ Speak positively about others. You will never regret the nice things you say about people.

She watches over the ways of her household, and does not eat the bread of idleness. Her children rise up and call her blessed; her husband also, and he praises her.

—Proverbs 31:27–28

381 ◆ Involve yourself so strongly with a charity or a cause that people easily associate it with you.

382 ◆ Volunteer to be the banker when playing Monopoly.

383 ◆ Show your children how to clothespin baseball cards to the spokes of their bikes to transform them into motorcycles.

384 ◆ Be more concerned about the direction of your life than its speed.

385 ◆ Attend a Memorial Day parade and salute every veteran who passes by.

386 ◆ When buying a new car or a new dress, remember you can't lose with the color red.

387 ◆ Never marry for money. You'll pay too much.

388 • Each week watch a couple of your children's favorite television programs with them.

389 • Greet family and friends with a "Home Sweet Home" sign hanging above your front door.

390 • When living alone, have an unlisted telephone number.

391 • Remember that the quality of your work is a snapshot of your character.

392 • Create a secure and consistent home environment for your children by setting and sticking to rules that let them know what is expected of them.

393 • Date many. Fall in love with few. Marry one.

394 • Take a family vacation every year, even if you spend it pitching a tent, tossing a Frisbee, and chasing butterflies.

395 • Remember that throughout life some pain is inevitable but misery is always optional.

396 • Teach your children how to lose as well as how to win.

397 • Change the water in fresh flower arrangements every other day.

398 • Don't forget that you and your husband are your children's most important teachers.

399 • Remember that life doesn't have to be perfect to be wonderful.

400 • Have a new college roommate every year. Each one will teach you more about relationships than you can learn anywhere else.

401 • Speak with enthusiasm when describing your husband, children, job, or employer, and give them reasons to do the same when describing you.

402 ◆ Remember that a good moral life never goes out of fashion.

403 ◆ Own beautifully personalized stationery. Use it often.

404 ◆ Realize that people will remember how you treated them long after they have forgotten what you were wearing.

405 • Remember that sometimes the nicest thing you can do for yourself is to do something nice for someone else.

406 • Ensure a successful marriage by falling in love over and over with your husband.

407 • Pay your credit card balances in full every month.

408 · Reserve your best behavior for your family, not for strangers.

409 • Remember that while you can't always be right, you can always be courteous.

410 • Learn to play a piano duet with your children, even if it's only an amateurish version of "Heart and Soul."

411 • Never speak negatively about one friend to another friend.

412 • Never enter your boss's office without a notepad and pencil.

413 • Find a perfume you love and be loyal to it.

414 • Always kiss your husband on New Year's Eve — even if you have to wake him up.

415 • Be an example of what you want to see more of in the world.

416 • Never focus on what you are not going
to do; focus instead on what you can and
will do.

417 • Remember that the style of your
handwriting speaks even before your
words do.

418 • When someone offers you a breath mint,
take it.

419 • Remember that everything that's questionable is easier to get into than out of.

420 • Don't waste time trying to make good deals with bad people.

421 • Take care of your reputation. There is nothing that takes a longer time to build or a shorter time to destroy.

422 ◆ Remain just a bit mysterious even to those who think they know everything about you.

423 ◆ When deciding matters of great importance, even after you think you have the answer, give it another twenty-four hours.

424 ◆ Remember that contentment is the greatest wealth.

425 • When traveling, think McDonald's when you need a clean restroom.

426 • Don't get romantically involved with anyone unless his inner beauty matches his outer beauty.

427 • Remember that home is the place where you love the most people.

428 · Bad things happen in bad places. So stay out of bad places.

429 ◆ Keep a diary of the significant moments in your life.

430 ◆ When scrapes and bruises occur, remember the healing power of a mother's kiss.

431 ◆ Fill your home with music. There are no happier children than those with songs in their hearts.

432 ◆ Never leave a message on your answering machine that would indicate that you might be out of town.

433 ◆ Regardless of the situation, react with class.

434 ◆ Spoil your husband, not your children.

435 ◆ Smile at all pregnant women.

436 • Remember, it's easier to meet the right person after you have become the right person.

437 • Hold hands with your family when saying grace.

438 • Spare no expense on your children's portraits; you will cherish them forever.

439. • If you have the honor of being in someone's wedding, send them an anniversary card every year.

440 • Live imaginatively.

441 • Listen patiently.

442 • Love trustingly.

443 • Always enjoy a corn dog at the county fair.

444 • Remember that wherever there are people, there are opportunities for kindness.

445 • Marry the man of your dreams. Never settle for less.

446 • Strive for a peaceful home, not a perfect one.

447 • Never forget how it feels to be sixteen.

448 • Always do your best.

449 • I know you will forget this, but try to remember that everything you do as a young girl, teenager, and adult is preparation for you to become the world's greatest mom.

Other Books by H. Jackson Brown, Jr.

A *Father's Book of Wisdom*
P.S. I Love You
Life's Little Instruction Book™ (volumes I, II, and III)
Live and Learn and Pass It On (volumes I, II, and III)
Wit and Wisdom from the Peanut Butter Gang
The Little Book of Christmas Joys
    (with Rosemary C. Brown and Kathy Peel)
A Hero in Every Heart (with Robyn Spizman)
Life's Little Treasure Books
    On Marriage and Family, On Wisdom, On Joy,
    On Success, On Love, On Parenting, Of Christmas Memories,
    Of Christmas Traditions, On Hope, On Friendship, On Fathers,
    On Mothers, On Things That Really Matter, On Simple Pleasures
Kids' Little Treasure Books
    On Happy Families
    On What We've Learned . . . So Far
Life's Instructions for Wisdom, Success, and Happiness
Life's Little Instructions from the Bible (with Rosemary C. Brown)
Life's Little Instruction Book™ *for Incurable Romantics* (with Robyn Spizman)
A Book of Love for My Daughter (with Kim Shea and Paula Y. Flautt)
A Book of Love for My Son (with Hy Brett)
Highlighted in Yellow (with Rochelle Pennington)